The Clear Path Home

God's Passionate Appeal to Win Your Heart

By

Jim Otis

authorHOUSE™

1663 Liberty Drive, Suite 200
Bloomington, Indiana 47403
(800) 839-8640
www.AuthorHouse.com